Quoetically Speaking

Quoetically Speaking

Isna Tianti

Atlanta, Ga

Quoetically Speaking
Copyright © 2017 Isna Tianti

All rights reserved.

No part of this book may be reproduced or transmitted in any form or by any means, electronic or mechanical, including photocopying, recording or by any information storage and retrieval system, without written permission from the publisher, except for the inclusion of brief quotations in a review.

Address inquiries to the publisher:

ITS Unlimited LLC
P.O. Box 1638
Atlanta, GA 30012

Learn more about the author at:
www.followisnat.com

ISBN: 978-0-9884906-4-2 (print)
ISBN: 978-0-9884906-2-8 (e-book)

Library of Congress Control Number: 2017944271

Revised and Edited By:
Tonya D. Zeigler
Yetmon Wright,
Elante Thomas
Nailah Summerlin

Final Interior Layout Formatted By:
Carlisa Flournoy and Tonya Zeigler

Printed in the United States of America

Dedication

To my father, King Allen C. Williams.
Thank you for your unconditional love, enduring friendship
and
transformative wisdom.

The beauty in traveling down the road less traveled is no
one can get in your way.

Acknowledgements
Introduction

Esteem 1

Inlightenment 11

Life Lessons 21

Love 31

Mental and Emotional Health 41

Nature 51

Quirky Quotes 61

Race Relations 71

Relationships 81

Religion and Spirituality 91

Time Management 101

Womb-n-Man 110

Quoetically Speaking

Acknowledgments

Writing acknowledgments is sometimes more complicated than writing the book itself. It requires an editor of a different calling to remember all the people who have made what I do possible in some form or fashion. First and foremost, I must give honor to The Most High, who created me. I refer to "The Most High" as such because I don't believe there is anything or one higher than the ONE who skillfully and wonderfully created me. I give thanks to my grandmother, Queen Georgia Glenn, who is my role model and friend. She passed on February 6, 2017 before her 91st birthday. Grandma, your wisdom shared lives on. To my late mother, Queen Darlene Ballard Anderson. Mommy, you spared your wings that I might fly. Your life has proven over time to be the first and last gift you gave to me. Thank you for carrying and cultivating me in your womb, giving me guidance, nourishment, compassion and love. I'm going to make every stretchmark you had due to birthing me count.

To my father, Allen C. Williams, King, I am so grateful for you daddy, and I am honored to have an unbreakable bond with you. Thank you, Ma Velma, for you being there through thick and thin. My stepfather Brian D. Anderson, thank you for giving me my maiden name, I love you for honoring us all to carry the "Anderson" name. What can I say about my three-beautiful seeds, Nailah, Tahira and Jahe. You are the best gift a mother could ask for! You all see and know every trial and triumph I've had to endure. You've seen countless tears from my physical pain, days when I stayed up late and still rose early. You saw every sacrifice, being disappointed, but rising higher when seemingly knocked down. Without hesitation, you would write down my quotes during conversations and while I drove. The three of you have been my right hand. Many of my quotes were written and inspired with you all in mind so that you would not have to hit the same brick walls I did. I am so proud of the young ladies and man you have become. If nothing else I can leave you, it is a legacy of quotes I wrote for you to take note of. Due to the GOD in you, I am the woman I am today.

My siblings by way of my mom: Diondra, Derek, and Solomon, you guys know where we came from. Mommy kept us together and taught us many lessons that I am honored and grateful to share. Mom would be proud of her tribe! Derek this hill would have been much more difficult to climb if you weren't the hand of support pushing me up. *Playtime Is Over* and I am eagerly awaiting that book to manifest. I appreciate you for all the years of support and belief in me. Solomon, *The Happy Health Squad* is on its way to success!

To my siblings by way of my father: Hyrone, Ebrahiem, Iziem, Anasa, Bahia, Malika, and Terrell, you will never be considered half of anything because you have my whole heart and love. Ahlumba Harris, my sis from another Mister and Miss; I am most grateful for you for helping me with the layout phase. I am so

Quoetically Speaking

grateful for you Lisa Molly for connecting me to Alicia Ward; you sisters are everything. Tonya Zeigler, thank you for always being so thoughtful in including me in The Bag Lady Experience Productions and assisting me with the revisions. You are a jewel!

To my godparents Ellen Foreman-Reese, Leo and Ana Soesman, Marjorie Oxford, Queen Ahneva Ahneva, and Ms. Olga. To my first chosen god-mother who transitioned Carol Irene Thomas, I'm still watching out for my sisters. You have all known me since my youth and early teen/adult years. You all have witnessed me tread through valleys and wade through overrunning streams in attempts to fulfill my dreams. You encouraged me to never give up during my journey. When my mother transitioned, I strongly believe she made it her parting mission to leave me with strong people like you. I am grateful to The Most High for you all.

To my first childhood friends I call my cousins by way of my Auntie Marjorie, Uncle Johnny, Uncle Danny, and Uncle Chester, thank you all for giving me a childhood and life full of great memories. My Olympian cousin Madeline Manning-Sims you are golden. My chosen friends from early elementary, middle and high school in order of first acquaintance: Karriema Samuel, Jennifer Miner, Stephanie Edwards, Shakenia H. Williams, Obadiah Cooper, Alvin Campbell, Paul Cooper, Monique Darby, and Denise Evans Claxton. You all kept me going with laughter, love and pure friendship when things got tough. My dearest Obie, thank you love for taking time to help me categorize my quotes and keeping my spirit uplifted. Your friendship is priceless. Althea Williams, Kim Lawrence, and Nadia E. your support and friendship were and is so instrumental in the completion of this book. My mentor, Jay White, what can I say KJ? You truly showed me that the "Hustle is Sold Separately!" I'm getting where I'm supposed to be, knowing my only competitor is me. Thank you, Hotep of Hustle University, for wanting only the best for me. I will utilize the ingredients in your books for advancing my success.

To all acknowledged, your belief in my gifts has made me walk in a bold, yet humble confidence. My god-sisters and brothers, Tanika Thomas, Laurren Bailey, Brian Walker, Illya, Omar, Emile, Jamila and Alisha Reese, Vanessa, Veronica, Vanda, (late) Noble Jr. Oxford. Thank you for sharing your parents with me.

My eternal gratitude to my re-editing and layout design team Tonya Zeigler, Carlisa Flournoy, Yetmon Wright, Elante Thomas and Nailah Summerlin., your willingness to pick up the broken pieces after the countless and unforeseen delays was medicine to my soul; your input was golden. To those who pre-ordered this book, thank you for your patience and understanding through all the delays. Beviyan Design Queen Wilson, your graphics are awesome; you did your thing with this cover. "B" tha Barber aka Sancarah Jackson, thanks for keeping my hair on point and all the meaningful talks in the shop. Hakim Wilson of Photo Brothers Media, thank you for the awesome photoshoot for my book cover and webpage. Ms. Nickee Mack with Diva Day International for my natural makeup artistry and awesome referrals. Cube57 for the beautiful blue dress that put the seal on the *inergy* I was feeling for this book. Natalya at Natalya's Beauty Supply, you not only supply me with my hair products, but you also give the best customer service with a smile. I love you all.

To Gayla Rogers, Latise Jordan, Michelle Boens, LaShea Burgess, and Tyrese Stafford, thanks for allowing me to be naked in vulnerability. Everyone should have a group of friends that they can call their naked group. I thank you Gayla, for taking my jewelry to Paris, LaShea for introducing the gratitude journal to me- it was life altering. Latise, you don't know how much it blessed me to hear you say I was like an *Oprah* in your eyes. Michelle, I'm waiting on your stage play. Tyrese, bro, thanks for your talks and introducing me to Chef Al Azzam and his beautiful wife Kimberly Hampton. I am grateful for all my Naya's Cafe experiences. I love you all.

Regina Sunshine, Shekema Silveri, Regina Breed, and Jack Tre of Instinct Radio, thank you for affording me a platform to utilize my journalistic skills. Who knew out the gate, I'd be interviewing such influential and prominent individuals in such a short time? My beautiful sister Paula G, Brian Richboi Joubert, and Klarque Garrison of the SRN family for having me on several shows for interviews and updates on my productivity. Love you so much. Ms. On Fire to Inspire, Aleigha Butler, thanks for having me on your show and sharing

Quoetically Speaking

your resources with me. For introducing me to Kristle Bledsoe and Angelice Washington two sisters who shared their gifts and talents with helping me. Stacy Douglas, thank you sister, for answering that call and extending the opportunity for me to share my spoken words on your platform.

Montoya Smith with *Mental Dialogue* for opening the lines of connection and communication. The Hank Stewart Foundation for inviting me to share my gift of spoken word on your many stages and motivating the youth each year for career day. Ric Mathis for creating the documentary *The Film Black Friday* and *The Remix*. You have changed how I look at conducting business and how I spend. That leads to the shout out to Eldredge E. Washington and Antwon Davis with *Spendefy*, the two of you have redefined how to expand the mind as it pertains to how we spend. Tarra Jackson aka MsMadamMoney for teaching me in your book, *Financial Fornication* that *Free* only means Fully Reimbursing Every Expense.

Felicitee Love, sistar, your spirit and future is grand. Kameelah Montgomery, thank you for challenging me to question truth. Ken Warner thanks for all the features and your support in my giftings'. Moody Black, collaborating with you was an epic moment. Bruce George, Founder of *Genius is Common* and Co- Founder of Def Poetry Jam, you inspired me to become the Quotologist I've become; Your *GIC!* Renata Brown, the visionary of GANSPA, I am grateful for your platform and my nomination for Best Female Poet of

Quoetically Speaking

2017. I applaud all the great and talented artists in that category. To my S-Word comrades Abyss, Jon Goode, Malik Salaam, Tommy Bottoms, Cola Rum, Queen Sheba, Nukola, Be'Nice, Bonnie Harvey, Theresa Da Songbird, Knyte Owens, Verbal Slick, NFared, Lauren Dorihana, I appreciate your dedication to the craft. Finally, Georgia Me, thanks for being an inspiration to writing one of my most requested spoken word pieces, *Loving Me, Loving You*. I became intentional about this GAME called LIFE and stopped taking my gifts for granted.

There are so many more poets and artists that have inspired me. However, I mentioned those who were on their grind when I came to Atlanta in 2004 and met within my first few years of taking to stages in GA. Although I was not a complete novice when I arrived on the scene, it was an unforgettable conversation with Queen Sheba at Club 908 who taught me the importance of committing to memory my spoken word. Thanks Queen. My Astro twin Lesley Hudson, you have shown me true sisterhood-we truly are two fish of a rare kind and find. Lol. I have learned in this artistry, we must unapologetically stay true to who we are.

Stephanie Brown, my sister, you took care of me when my pain was so intense, stopping everything to make sure I was well. Thanks so much! To my fellow VA Women Warriors and facilitators, y'all know y'all my girls, who will always remain close to my heart! You help me more than you'll ever know. Gameli Appiah, your friendship was the breath of fresh air I needed to be revived. Charles Freeman, my mother's astro-twin and my new "IG" friend who inspired me to the end; much appreciation.

To all my associates and acquaintances, my experiences with you have taught me countless lessons. Some lessons I had to learn the hard way. I had to see that friendships like anything else need readjusting in an effort to grow. We must be mindful that even though we outgrow relationships-we must not throw away the lessons learned. Letting go isn't always a negative thing. At this juncture in my life, quality will always override quantity.

My nieces and nephews– so many to name – this book is written for you to reference whenever you need a word from Auntie Isna. You all truly are my heart and I am expecting greatness from you.

To all my ancestors and friends who have transitioned that impacted or influenced my life in a grand way, I feel your presence with me every day. Rest In Power: Great-great grandmother Estella Freeman, Great-grandmother Janie Ballard, Grandma Earnestine, Aunt Betty, Uncle Linton, Uncle Earl (Bubba), my cousin, former Mayor of Cleveland, Carl Stokes and former Ambassador-Congressman Louis Stokes. My buddie Milton Harris who taught me early how a real man leaves a legacy by their deeds. To the late, great Dr. Maya Angelou, "My Spiritual Momma Maya," Thanks for planting an anointed kiss on my cheek on January 11, 2007. Your legacy carries on. Though I never met

Quoetically Speaking

these Queens- Harriet Tubman, Sojourner Truth and Nina Simone they keep me grounded to walk and speak my truth. Queen India Arie you are my modern day musical inspiration and possess the inergy of the three I for mentioned, your spirit gives me light and life. To these Kings whose music I seek for inspiration as I write, THE Legendary John Coltrane, Miles Davis and still amongst us Pharoah Sanders, and last but not least musical genius and my inspiration King Stevie Wonder, you have been a major "key in my life!" Your lyrics opened the pathway and door to my passion for reading and writing poetry since the age of 5. Thank you so much for gracing the world with your gifts. You are *A Ribbon in My Ebony Eyes!* I pray this book makes you all proud.

If by chance your name was omitted, and you know without a shadow of doubt you have shared your life, love and time with me, please charge it to my head and not my heart.

Introduction

When given the mandate to write this book, *Quoetically Speaking*, I knew that this was a divine assignment. For such a time as this, I believe I was aligned to write these quotes. The late, great Nina Simone put it so eloquently, "An artist's duty, as far as I'm concerned, is to reflect the times." In concurrence with Queen Nina Simone, I felt compelled to complete the task of putting my thoughts regarding today's times in poetic quotes, hence, the title's compilation.

Quoetically Speaking infuses my love of writing poetry with creating quotes. Inspired by an acronym that I composed a few years ago for the word LIFE (Lessons In Form of Experiences)-this is one of the premises for the book. Life will hand us many lessons in the form of experiences, and either we will learn from the experiences or keep repeating them until we do. Much like school, we can't be promoted to the next level until we have mastered the skills necessary to pass life's most challenging tests.

As you read each quote, I want you to read, re-read, and ponder them. Allow your spirit to marinate on what is being said. Some quotes will most likely make you laugh, smile, or have an Ashe, Selah, Amen and *Awomen* reaction. Your belief system, thought process, and willingness to be open will all be challenged. If none of the above occurs, then I will have not fulfilled my purpose for writing these quotes. However, if we are honest with ourselves, we can all stand to have our thinking in at least one of the 12 chapters challenged or our perceptions adjusted to some degree.

My goal is to never cause anyone to falter or stumble in their faith or beliefs because those are often the very foundation on which we stand. My goal is, however, to evoke questions and increase awareness. If nothing in life ever stays the same, why do we concede that our belief systems should remain stagnant or rarely change? Important questions we want answered often go unanswered because they are rarely asked.

When we read something, we are made to feel as if we have to accept it or deny it based on what we've been previously taught or, better yet, not taught at all. If something doesn't resonate with our spirit, we often see no value in accepting it. What we do not realize is that new thoughts, like a new pair of shoes, have to be broken into. Once they expand, much like our thinking, our feet can comfortably walk in that newfound truth or idea. It isn't until we tap into how we feel about a certain subject matter, that we can be real with ourselves and others. We need to evaluate or re-evaluate if the foundations we stand on are founded on and rooted in truth.

Quoetically Speaking is filled with quotes that will challenge you to think outside the box and question norms, asking why we have been conditioned to think only one way.

Quoetically Speaking

As you read further, you will notice that I have modified the spelling of some words to cause you to see them from a different perspective, giving them more power and taking away their negative or limited connotations. Even the name of the book offers poetic word play. In recreating words, I take one or more words and make them look the way I see them in my head. If the English language can include words like there, their, they're and two, too, and to, then I can write "thare and tue." The mind is vast, and it processes our thoughts in many colors, scents, feelings and sounds. Not only is recreating new words exciting, but what I attempt to do when I choose to alter a word is have you also see its alternative meaning.

My mission is to give new "inergy" to old words that are often overlooked or no longer serve their original connotation. I challenge you to not just read these quotes, but also read them with an open mind to see something different than you did previously.

Ultimately, Quoetically Speaking should inspire you to ponder your experiences in life and create a few quotes of your own based on your personal experiences. Life and nature are our two best teachers. So much can be learned from simply observing nature and those who interact in it. That said, many of these quotes are inspired by either of the two.

Inspiration of Symbols Chosen

Color Blue
Blue is the color of the sky and oceans. It is often associated with stability, depth, loyalty, wisdom, confidence, intelligence, faith, truth, heaven, and it symbolizes trust.

Number 12
It represents the completed cycle of experience and when an individual reincarnates as the number 12, they have completed a full cycle of experience and learned of the possibility of regeneration toward a higher consciousness. It belongs to a group of developed souls who have acquired an unusual inner strength through many and varied lifetimes. The soul attracts what it needs as a learning experience. The number 12 represents the educational process on all levels, the submission of the will required, and the sacrifice necessary to achieve knowledge and wisdom on both spiritual and intellectual levels.

Blue Butterflies
Blue Butterflies can be diverse. They are often seen as a sign of life. They symbolize change or rebirth, regardless of their color. Blue butterflies represent symbols of love. Blue is one of the freshest colors. Due to their colors, blue butterflies send vibrations of joy and happiness. Blue butterflies are considered wish granters.

Dragonflies
Similar to butterflies, dragonflies symbolize transformation and rebirth. In some Native American traditions, they also symbolize departed souls. Dragonflies are associated with the Mayan animal symbol of the goddess of creativity, the guard of our dreams, as well they represent us seeking out our true potential and the ability for us to manifest our birthright. The wings of dragonflies reflect the colors of the Universe and connects us to its *inergy*.

Blue Phoenix Bird
The phoenix is said to be a mythological bird that recycles its own life. When it perceives its impending death, the phoenix transforms itself into a brilliant fire. In time, it reemerges from its own ashes - reborn, renewed, and very much alive.

Quoetically Speaking

Quoetically Speaking

1

Esteem

Never let anyone suppress or press the esteem out of you, be who you are no matter what anyone says or does.

I'm never intimidated by others' success because I don't see myself as less.

1-2; 11:58 am

Pain is a part of the process of birthing someone and something *Behuetiful*.

1-9; 9:40 am

Know thy worth and value, and no one can ever sell you short.

1-10; 8:38 am

Your gifts are a present to the world. That's why you were presented to the world.

1-14; 9:14 am

My journey takes roads your GPS would never find.

1-14; 9:27 am

Quoetically Speaking

Insecurities are like unwanted guests you allow in your house. In order to have inward peace you have to put those negative feelings out.

1-14; 10:57 am

We're all predisposed for greatness; it's just some of us never expose it.

1-16; 5:10 pm

Attempt it again and again, not giving up is the only way you'll win.

1-18; 7:25 am

I *incourage* so I won't be discouraged.

1-18; 10:25 am

I'm aware that I'm unique, and that will never be something I'll let you take from me.

1-18; 1:53 pm

My boundaries are well guarded, so before crossing them, know I'm bound to defend them to the fullest extent.

1-18; 1:55 pm

Quoetically Speaking

Scared of what? Scared of who? You can kill my flesh but what else can you do?

1-20; 7:49 am

Though many fears are warranted; don't let them arrest you.

1-20; 8:01 am

Can't make it any clearer, but we must first start with the one standing in the mirror.

1-20; 8:06 am

Change is in your pockets; so put your hands in the process if you want to see how it looks and feels.

1-20; 8:07 am

Inspiration begins with a spark from within.

1-20; 11:44 am

Sports can be compared to scoring in life – no work no pay.

1-20; 4:49 pm

Someone can drive you where you want to go, but you must be driven to meet your own goals.

1-22; 8:13 am

Quoetically Speaking

No one can make you move, but someone can make you **MO**ti**V**at**E**e**D** to move.

1-22; 8:16 am

When you find yourself being idle, get in gear and get moving.

1-22; 9:46 am

Your esteem, like steam, should always rise when you find yourself in heat.

1-22; 10:57 am

Profess to be greater than great, and watch the levies break
.
1-22; 11:21 am

Meeting a goal's only purpose is for us to ask ourselves, "What's next?"

1-22; 11:39 am

No one is responsible for our choices but our own inner voices.

1-23; 11:44 am

Quoetically Speaking

Tell me your net worth and I'll show my soul is worth more than your assets or cash.

1-24; 12:35 am

Explain how complaining has ever won anyone an award for best speech!

1-24; 2:15 am

Never fear who'll be the last ones standing, for the resiliency of one born in struggle is uncanny.

1-24; 10:01 am

You can't give a mirror as a gift without first looking in it.

1-24; 10:44 am

A wealthy person's best friend is often their ego.

1-24; 12:39 am

Every person we value as less has a place in history.

1-25; 8:12 am

Being ashamed and being a shame is not the same.

1-25; 8:37 am

Quoetically Speaking

Be the proof you are alive and not just living.
1-25; 9:31 am

Don't try to convince anyone but yourself that you were born on purpose to have success and nothing less.

1-25; 9:32 am

In order to leave a legacy, you've got to walk in your calling.

1-25; 9:33 am

You don't need legs to leave a legacy. You only need heart to do your part.

1-25; 9:34 am

All it takes is vision and a strong will to fulfill your dreams.

1-25; 9:35 am

The Most High created enough sons and daughters for us all to shine without casting shade.

1-25; 9:55 am

A thought not written will eventually fade away like seconds in a day.

1-25; 10:12 am

Quoetically Speaking

The only way you'll change what you get is when you change what you do.

1-25; 10:15 am

If you never begin, you will never know the outcome in the end.

6-24; 10:55 pm

Quoetically Speaking

Reflection

Quoetically Speaking

**❛❛ *Never* let anyone suppress or press the esteem out of you, be who you are no matter what anyone says or does.* ❜❜

2
Inlightenment

When we are inlightened, our world is brightened with an illuminous glow, because we are now in the know spiritually and mentally.

When they spoke, I questioned no more.

1- 6; 3:06 pm

Disappointment is only a temporary missed appointment with satisfaction.

1-8; 4:45 pm

Your happiness should never be contingent on what happens.

1-8; 4:48 pm

Fear must pass from being our favorite pastime.

1-8; 4:53 pm

The eyes have seen stories that the mouth can never tell.

1-13; 12:23 am

Quoetically Speaking

Four wheels, a steering wheel and engine gets everyone to the same destination.

1-14; 9:00 am

A mouth says many things, but a wise one chooses carefully.

1-14; 9:01 am

Having money without wisdom is like having teeth to eat but no tongue.

1-14; 9:16 am

Having sight but no vision is like having a mansion built with no windows.

1-14; 9:19 am

People want change but don't have one cent of sense.

1-14; 10:49 am

Those who scheme to fulfill their dreams, prepare for a nightmare.

1-14; 11:04 am

Writing the vision down doesn't mean it'll be done right now.

1-14; 11:55 am

Quoetically Speaking

We all have dreams that seem unreal until we wake up
and realize they can become our reality.

1-15; 1:49 am

Tell me there's only one way, and I'll show you a globe.

1-15; 1:54 am

A closed mouth may not get fed, but it sure will leave
your enemy guessing what's going on inside your head.

1-16; 2:16 am

If you're the best, what about all the rest who have
reached equal or greater success?

1-16; 2:20 am

Children at play don't play around when playing on the
play- ground.

1-16; 5:05 pm

Your fears are as real as you make them out to be.

1-16; 7:11 pm

I still see when my eyes are shut tight; I have vision
beyond mere sight.

1-17; 7:20 am

Quoetically Speaking

Even rich people lose money and their touch to manipulate a facade of power.

1-17; 1:40 pm.

Avoidance of a question is not an answer.

1-18; 2:10 pm

A mirror can never reflect your soul, just as a plate can never be a bowl.

1-20; 12:37 pm

I have more respect for the blind who read Braille, than for those with sight who fail to see that they're blind as hell.

1-20; 2:08 pm

I dare one more person to criticize Stevie Wonder's hairline, when many are standing on the sideline doing squat
for mankind.

1-20; 2:14 pm

Everyone who has sight doesn't have insight.

1-22; 8:18 am

Quoetically Speaking

Giving someone the pen to write your testimony is plagiarism.

1-24; 12:12 am

A rich person gets buried just like the poor person – Alone.

1-24; 12:40 am

The poor have more inspiration to create with a spoon than those born with a silver one in their mouth.

1-24; 9:59 am

We can't show anyone their faults when we fail to see our own.

1-24; 7:34 pm

Most times we don't suffer from a lack of knowledge, but misinformation we've come to know and apply.

1-25; 7:14 am

A baby is like a new computer, we can download anything onto their hard drive and it will be the basis of what drives them.

1-25; 7:22 am

Quoetically Speaking

With moving fingers, a computer mouse that clicks, has become the norm of socializing, choosing mates and forming online cliques.

1-25; 8:28 am

A dream deferred is preferred by your enemy.

1-25; 10:12 am

Greedy people will even view others' pain as their gain.

1-25; 10:17 am

Many desire for peace to come, but how can it if we keep killing our young?

1-25; 10:22 am

Walking and Talking are both action words, but one out of the two gets things done and it isn't the one that can be heard.

1-25; 10:35 am

How am I expected to pull myself up by my bootstraps and tie them with wet noodles for strings?

1-25; 1:26 pm

Quoetically Speaking

Print your photos so your existence isn't considered a negative lie.

1-25; 1:35 pm

Material things don't make us more than or less, they just make more of a cluttered mess.

1-25; 1:42 pm

Wise people never ask who shot the gun. Their instinct automatically tells them to run.

1-25; 1:50 pm

Reflection

Quoetically Speaking

❝ When we are ***inlightened***, *our world is brightened with an illuminous glow, because we are now in the know spiritually and mentally.* ❞

3
Life Lessons

***Life will teach you an abundance of things, but you must
remember to be mindful of the lessons they bring.***

When we just sit, we'll never be fit to get what we're to get.

1-4; 10:01 am

Arrogance is not a prerequisite for intelligence.

1-2; 11:50 am

Our character should never be misconstrued with being a caricature.

1-6; 8:48 am

When you work hard at hurting others, payday is a hefty paycheck called "karma."

1-8; 3:49 pm

What we need most should be what we want most.

1-8; 4:56 pm

The strongest of people cry, even if it's in the form of sweat.

1-11; 10:19 am

We all need to find our own lane and stay in it. Maybe if we did, we'd have less fatalities; blocking traffic flow because we don't know what we want to do or where we want to go.

1-13; 8:25 am

You won't drown because you failed at learning how to swim, but because you didn't try to get in.

1-13; 10:05 am

Life is like shooting an arrow. Sometimes we miss the mark.

1-14; 10:42 am

What you desire can be acquired, but you won't get it if you easily tire.

1-14; 11:02 am

Saying the word "try" is like trying to pick up a pen and write; either you do it or you don't.

1-14; 12:33 pm

Quoetically Speaking

Subjects we study and learn are always subjective.

1-14; 12:37 pm

It doesn't make it true just because someone says it's so.
It becomes truth when we trust and instinctively know.

1-15; 1:51 am

Convince, convert, and condition all try to CONfuse
people into switching their mind's position.

1-15; 2:08 am

I agree; let your "yes" be "yes," but your "no" is the real test.

1 16; 2:18 am

If you strike a match, prepare to put a fire out.

1-16; 5:03 pm

The answer will either be a yes or no, but if you fear
asking, you'll never know.

1-16; 7:10 pm

If you're going to tattle, then tell the whole damn truth.

1-17; 1:00 pm

Quoetically Speaking

Giving up and giving in will never work in this race called life we're in.

1-18; 3:10 pm

Change begins with pennies, quarters, nickels, and dimes, and it can make a big impact if everyone contributed positively a little at a time.

1-20; 8:11 am

The lesson in watching someone else receive an award shows that we all have the ability to win.

1-20; 11:42 am

Don't be swift to kick up dirt on someone else because the dust will rest upon you.

1-20; 12:34 pm

If this land is your land and this land is my land, when will I get the deed saying "Paid in Full" in hand?

1-20; 3:55 pm

Execute your excuses execution style.

1-24; 1:04 am

Quoetically Speaking

Excuses are like pennies on the ground; you look for them and one is bound to be found.

1-24; 9:41 am

Can people really call it complaining when they are really explaining?

1-24; 10:06 am

People can't buy drugs unless they are provided for them to pay.

1-24; 1:44 pm

The same mistake can only be made once; after that it's a choice.

1-24; 1:45 pm

Is a condescending smile really a smile at all?

1-24; 7:26 pm

If a smile turns into a frown a second after given, it's likely to be fake.

1-24; 7:26 pm

Quoetically Speaking

Pretentious Pretenders all come beforehand, intending to make you watch in defense.

1-24; 7:27 pm

Plan to deceive and see what grows from that seed.

1-26; 10:00 am

Walking on eggshells can still cut your feet.

1-26; 10:01 am

The war has and will always be on the shores where we first open our own doors.

1-28; 12:33 pm

The dreams you dream will fade if you don't write them when you wake.

1-30; 6:49am

Having money separate from wisdom is like removing the numbers off dollar bills.

1-30; 7:00 am

Never brag about your success, let your admirers say that you're the best.

1-30; 7:04 am

Quoetically Speaking

Does anyone truly win in a race war?

1-30; 7:10 am

If your motives are pure, then your moves of success are sure.

1-30; 7:16 am

A beautiful sandcastle can be built, but its soft foundation is sure to erode.

1-30; 9:22 am

Quoetically Speaking

Reflection

Quoetically Speaking

66 *Life* *will teach you an abundance of things, but you must remember to be mindful of the lessons they bring.* **99**

4
Love

Love is an action that moves and feels. It should evoke and emit a positive vibe, yet love can only be given if it resides inside to be considered real.

Once love finds us, we can never lose it, for it dwells inside.

1-1; 6:48 am

When you find GOD, you find you and Love.

1-1; 6:50 am

Love solves the equation for hate.

1-2; 11:57 am

Love evolves only when we resolve to stop hate.

1-8; 5:00 pm

Music is therapy for the soul that can start with singing yourself a song.

1-14; 8:56 pm

Your hand in my hand doesn't allow me to stand over or beneath you, but beside you.

1-16; 5:06 pm

Being happy won't happen, unless you choose to be the 'I' in happIness.

1-18; 9:00 am

Love me for me or let me be. I'm not here to fulfill your fantasies.

1-18; 1:51 pm

I can't fall in love with anyone not willing to catch me when I fall.

1-19; 11:35 am

Apologizing is acknowledging you crossed the fence of offense.

1-19; 11:52 am

You don't have to tell me you're sorry; just apologize for showing me your true character.

1-19; 11:53 am

Quoetically Speaking

Just looking at a book will never get one hooked.

1-20; 11:45 am

If you want to impress me, talk with your hands and feet.

1-20; 12:48 pm

Blood may be thicker than water, but blood isn't healthy to drink.

1-22; 8:04 am

I don't get even, even when I'm mad.

1-22; 8:09 am

Hurt should never cause anyone to bury another under dirt.

1-22; 8:12 am

See what I'm saying with your ears; feel what I'm saying with your heart.

1-22; 8:21 am

If you ask for a woman's hand in marriage, it's only fair you release it when you feel it no longer seems to fit.

1-22; 8:22 am

Kiss me tenderly, long and soft, but not with deceitful lips.

1-22; 8:40 am

If others fail to reciprocate what you need to thrive, self-preservation is a must for you to stay alive.

1-22; 9:23 am

Yes, family blood is thicker, but if tainted, it can make you sicker.

1-22; 10:09 am

Love is not an emotionless emotion; it is emotions put in motion.

1-22; 10:48 am

Love is like a caterpillar; the stages evolve into a beautiful butterfly over time.

1-22; 10:54 am

Give me gardenias because most don't seem to smell the roses in their life.

1-23; 12:06 am

Quoetically Speaking

Don't mistake my ears or heart for your trash can.

1-24; 2:08 am

When I trust you to open my heart, it's equivalent to seeing the red sea part.

1-24; 2:09 am

Has anyone thanked our mail carriers, who for years were chased by dogs to deliver our mail to us?

1-24; 10:11 am

Don't treat people the way you'd want to be treated if you don't love yourself.

1-24; 7:33 pm

Never make a promise, for we can only possess pure intent.

1-24; 7:42 pm

If like produces like, maybe that's why we can't seem to get this love thing right.

1-27; 2:59 pm

Quoetically Speaking

No one wants to be the last one standing in love alone.

1-27; 3:06 pm

Be very clear about who you are, don't be opaque.

1-30: 6:51 am

Your reflection should be the same once you leave the mirror.

1-30; 6:53 am

Don't forget who you are just because you can no longer see your reflection.

1-30; 6:53 am

Mirrors don't change the reflection just because you don't like what it reflects.

1-30; 6:54 am

A camera can only capture what it sees.

1-30; 6:55 am

Quoetically Speaking

I know The Most High loves me so; I see, feel, hear, smell and touch ITS existence everywhere I go.

1-30; 7:01 am

Trusting others first begins when we learn to trust ourselves.

1-30; 7:04 am

You'll never have to chase love if it comes knocking at your door.

1-30; 7:05 am

Loving and knowing you is the best gift you can give yourself.

1-30; 7:16 am

Reflection

Quoetically Speaking

❝Love is an action that moves and feels. It should evoke and emit a positive vibe, yet love can only be given if it resides inside to be considered real. ❞

5
Mental & Emotional Health

Our minds were uniquely designed to be free, one of a kind, and never confined. The only way it will remain intact and at peace is if we refuse to let others dissect it piece by piece.

We want to move to a different 'State' for change, but still take with us the same 'state of mind'. We'll only find the same problems in a different state if we don't first change our state of thinking instead of our address.

1-1; 6:45 am

The only baggage I'm packing is to take on a trip, not because I keep tripping.

1-1; 6:47 am

If we are what we consume, some of us need to detox every day.

1-6; 8:58 am

The cure for Post-Traumatic Stress (PTS): is giving the mind peace and rest.

1-6; 3:12 pm

Pain will not stain or skew my view on what I was sent to do.

1-9; 10:03 am

Oftentimes, our worst enemy is our inner-me, which must first be dealt with inwardly.

1-10; 8:40 am

Being tired can come from working out and being worked over.

1-14; 9:06 am

When you see you're running out of space, go to the next line.

1-16; 5:04 pm

Some people are dead even with a beating heart.

1-16; 3:08 pm

Quoetically Speaking

Dishonesty is like being bitten by ticks. Think of liars like Lyme disease, both will make you sick.

1-17; 1:10 pm

Whatever you've gone through was merely to get you to another destination.

1-18; 7:32 am

Lies like flies I despise. They blind me with aggravation and anger, like bleach thrown in my eyes.

1-19; 9:45 am

Instead of saying "no pun intended," be real and say "truth intended."

1-20; 12:57 pm

Unless you give me the tools to unscrew these screws, I'm screwed!

1-20; 1:41 pm

Show me mental illness, and I'll show you a creative, brilliant soul and mind.

1-20; 1:55 pm

God must be bipolar. He's always up and down and never asleep.

1-20; 1:57 pm

The label of being 'mentally disturbed' is only a name used by those disturbed to describe the 'mentally misunderstood.'

1-20; 1:59 pm

What's the difference between a person who avoids truth and a sleep walker? Nothing. They're both unaware they are walking and not awake.

1-20; 5:37 pm

Being sharp doesn't mean we have to cut.

1-22; 11:15 am

Nature is bipolar, hot one day and cold the next. It has animals and humans daily pining for sex.

1-22; 12:36 pm

Exhausted people have no energy to exhaust.

1-23; 11:49 am

Quoetically Speaking

Breathe and catch your breath before it becomes a fading memory of your past.

1-24; 12:04 am

If everyone was blessed to have what they need, there'd be no need for greed.

1-24; 12:16 am

Radically eradicate your fears.

1-24; 1:05 am

Many are dedicated to fear like a first love.

1-24; 1:06 am

Don't blame poor choices on your past.

1-24; 1:48 pm

Poor Choices = Poor Outcomes.

1-24; 1:49 pm

Assuming the worst first is usually the result of growing accustomed to being treated the worst.

1-24; 7:32 pm

Quoetically Speaking

Rest is necessary, for even God rested on the seventh day.

1-24; 7:40 pm

If you're weary, you'll either rest temporarily or rest permanently.

1-24; 7:41 pm

Don't confuse Know for No - you need to know when I say No…I'm not saying Know.

1-27; 6:58 am

There are boundaries and borderlines everyone walks on and over but should never break.

1-27; 7:03 am

Stay away from GMO's - Generically Modified Offenders who pretend to be your man and friends.

1-27; 8:01 am

Some are still broke after selling their souls for a mouth & neck full of gold.

1-27: 7:43 pm

Quoetically Speaking

People are dying trying to get rich while their mind is still broke & sick.

1-27; 7:45 pm

Our wealth and richness can never heal sickness.

1-27; 7:46 pm

Don't let the wrong head get you misled - many lives have been destroyed by both.

1-30; 6:57 am

Love is bare, naked and undressed; covering and hiding nothing, even our brokenness.

1-30; 7:11 am

My loving you isn't contingent on whether you love me back.

1-30; 7:12 am

Reflection

Quoetically Speaking

*“Our **minds** were uniquely designed to be free, one of a kind, and never confined. The only way it will remain intact and at peace is if we refuse to let others dissect it piece by piece.”*

6
Nature

Nature teaches us so many valuable things and we can learn by watching seasons, how we evolve just like winter, summer, fall and spring.

Like trees, people need the sun and rain to grow; but why do we, unlike trees, compete, I'll never know.

1-14; 11:12 am

If leaves don't try to compete with a tree, leave me be if you feel you must compete with me.

1-18; 3:00 pm

Why don't bees' sting butterflies? Maybe out of respect that they're both meant to share the same skies and fly.

1-18; 3:02 pm

Sometimes I wish Mother Nature would teach humankind a class on how to nurture.

1-18; 3:05 pm

Even busy bees take time to smell the flowers.

1-19; 8:17 am

Turtles are my heroes. Although slow, they still get where they want to go.

1-19; 8:18 am

Whales may be big as hell, but without fail they keep swimming amongst smaller and cuter fish.

1-19; 8:18 am

Birds inspire me. They can make their home in a bush or tree and still fly free.

1-19; 8:20 am

Ants are amazing; as little as they might be, they are the best examples of black unity.

1-19; 8:25 am

People deal with truth like flies. Either we'll kill or swat them away, despise them, or accept them and let them fly as they may.

1-19; 9:51 am

Quoetically Speaking

Hey! At the end of the day, it's the end of the day.

1-20; 7:58 am

A plant can't tell you but will show you that it feels neglected.

1-20; 11:46 am

Babies cry because they can't express the how, when, what, where, and why.

1-20; 11:47 am

The end never ends because time begins again and again.

1-20; 11:59 am

Observe Mother Nature, for her nature will show you how to behave.

1-22; 9:01 am

Not all birds fly in flocks.

1-22; 9:01 am

A tree will teach you how to be still, bend with the wind and yet stay rooted.

1-22; 10:25 am

Quoetically Speaking

Trust what you believe like a farmer when they plant a seed.

1-22; 10:30 am

I'd rather face a mother bear rather than a police officer who doesn't care.

1-22; 12:25 pm

An elephant never forgets the path they take, leaving deep impressions on the journey they make.

1-22; 12:29 pm

Show me a snail and I'll show you one who will keep moving until you throw salt in its path.

1-23; 7:29 pm

Being raised and reared clearly isn't the same if you act like a wolf.

1-23; 7:35 pm

We can't do anything excessively all day except breathe.

1-23; 7:38 pm

Quoetically Speaking

Mourning is a normal way we grieve-will others mourn when you leave?

1-24; 12:09 am

Mistakes will inevitably be made, but habits are another thing.

1-24; 1:46 pm

Fret for what? We're all going to either live or die.

1-24; 7:42 pm

Be careful of the seeds you plant- you may have to eat that fruit one day.

1-26; 10:10 am

People truly believe only in what they see- many would doubt the bible if they took everything literally.

1-26; 10:12 am

Question everything or nothing & you still may never know.

1-27; 7:23 am

Work quickly and quietly so your enemy can't hinder your productivity.

1-27; 1:30 pm

If all lives matter, why does saying black lives matter disturb most of you, doesn't all include black lives too?

1-27; 1:32 pm

Naturally, people aren't colorblind; many just refuse to remove their blinders so that they can see.

1-27; 1:33 pm

So, Wait! We are going to ruin the world trying to rule a world which we didn't or can't create?

1-27; 1:35 pm

The weapons plotted to kill Mother Nature- will ultimately reverse.

1-27; 1:36 pm

What you do and say doesn't just go away; karma has a way of showing up for pay day.

1-27; 1:39 pm

Quoetically Speaking

Pay attention to detail, or you'll pay and fail for not doing so.

1-30; 6:50 am

When people get money they only show you the hidden treasures of their heart.

1-30; 6:59 am

Those who doubt truth as being a lie, are usually the same ones who deny the gigantic speck in their eye.

1-30; 7:02 am

The very nature of love is peculiar, yet it never forces itself on you.

1-30; 7:07 am

The Universe is already aligned, we just need to fine tune our time and mind.

1-30; 9:10 am

Reflection

Quoetically Speaking

*“ **Nature** teaches us so many valuable things and we can learn by watching seasons, how we evolve just like winter, summer, fall and spring. ”*

7
Quirky Quotes

I have an unusual mind that is truly set a part. Although each quote was written by inspiration, some are just quirky thoughts in my mind and heart. So, if any should offend due to how I expressed my thoughts, I ask that you hold no ought.

From airplanes, all houses and cars look the same.

1-14: 8:59 am

Trying to force a gay person to be straight is like making a red-blooded American eat a steak without a potato.

1-14; 10:46 am

If so above is so below, if hatred exists in heaven, I'm not sure I want to go.

1-16; 9:18 am

I've never seen a newborn rob, steal or kill, so to be born a sinner was not The Most High's will.

1-16; 5:11 pm

Quoetically Speaking

Any dog will holler if you yank and pull its collar.

1-17; 12:55 pm

Pussycats can get fleas sleeping around dogs.

1-17; 12:56 pm

Opinions are like onions. There are many layers, but I still may think yours stink.

1-18; 3:11 pm

For those addicted to playing *Call of Duty*, your duty is to find your call.

1-18; 10:14 pm

I guarantee if freedom of speech wasn't free, social media alone would be a multi-bi-zillion dollar entity.

1-19; 8:31 am

Not seeing my call on your call log doesn't mean it wasn't made.

1-19; 9:01 am

Cellphones have caused more problems than the calls they make.

1-19; 9:04 am

Quoetically Speaking

Unlocked phones have caused more crimes than unlocked homes.

1-19; 9:05 am

Black Sharpies, like black people are sharp. They aren't easily erased, and on the world have made a permanent and lasting mark.

1-19; 9:28 am

I've never seen a white marker make a mark on all-white paper that throughout school we've been made to use; I have, however, seen whites leave black and red marks on black backs from years of being beaten and abused.

1-19; 9:32 am

If we are to watch what we eat and with whom we sleep, how do we keep from eating and sleeping with Monsanto's GMO hoes?

1-19; 9:47 am

I wish Brinks could protect cell phones as well as it does homes.

1-19; 10:14 am

I wish there was a fine for the crime of intruders invading my personal space, such disrespect all up in my face.

1-19; 10:16 am

If lawyers and judges had to serve time, what would be their sentence or fine for sending people to jail for a nonexistent crime?

1-19; 10:19 am

Like water, justice can't be frozen to justICE.

1-19; 10:21 am

Judges, in court, sentence people for petty to hard crimes. Well it appears to me, if like recognizes like, who but a judge can comprehend a criminal's mind?

1-19; 10:39 am

People give way too much credit to our judicial system that systematically continues to fail.

1-20; 7:56 am

Read what was read to see that what he read wasn't what he meant to read – complexities of American literacy.

1-20; 9:10 am

Quoetically Speaking

Show me a person who has never cursed who you know, and let me drop a brick on their big toe.

1-20; 1:02 pm

I have little sympathy for a person with a sound mind and sight who refuses to learn how to read and write.

1-20; 2:02 pm

Stevie Wonder made me wonder what his world was like, and he is one of my biggest inspirations that has propelled me to write.

1-20; 2:05 pm

Fear is not a factor in the equation of my life.

1-24; 12:11 am

Lotto or Lie-though: The money supposedly goes to our schools-miss me with that lie bro!

1-24; 12:34 am

I can't take bread to the bank or eat money when my belly growls.

1-24; 9:44 am

Quoetically Speaking

Intentions are fine, but I'm just partial to the ones that are followed through.

1-24; 9:42 am

Make no mistake; joining the military is unlike any other job most take. We get paid to put our lives on the line when your freedoms are at stake.

1-24; 10:07 am

Let go of your ego- No, I didn't say your Eggo.

1-27; 6:51 am

I walk on top of water every time I shower.

1-27: 7:04 am

If GOD is said to be good ALL the time and the word GOoD has GOD's name in it just with an extra O; GOD looked at what He created and said 'IT IS GOoD' then it still must be so.

1-27; 7:10 am

What earthly judge or jury can separate and define sentencing anyone to serve lifetime for a petty crime, if we all have sinned?

1-27; 7:28 am

Quoetically Speaking

I can give you my pledge of Sponsorship, but I refuse to give my time to sponsor-ur-shyt.

1-27; 2:50 pm

A woman shouldn't be despised just because she refuses to lay and have her eggs fertilized; she's not to be deemed a chicken just because she has legs, breasts, and thighs.

1-27; 3:01 pm

Dare! Don't be scared to be different.

1-27; 3:02 pm

White has always been associated with everything right, but how is it that everything wrong has happened in The White House which is the only thing in that neighborhood that appears pristine and bright.

1-28; 11:44 pm

I want love to be like night and day when it comes, I want it to just sneak up on me as I'm doing what needs to be done.

1-30: 7:09 am

If your motives and intents are pure, doubt not, your success is sure.

1-30; 7:09 am

Reflection

Quoetically Speaking

*❝I have an unusual mind that is truly set a part. Although each quote was written by **inspiration**, some are just quirky thoughts in my mind and heart. So, if any should offend due to how I expressed my thoughts, I ask that you hold no ought. ❞*

8
Race Relations

Race relations is the talk of the hour. Like a relationship gone south; it's stale and sour. We must fight against these evils and relinquish its power.

Refuse, rebuke and refute ignorance, for we must not recycle or rewind this rubbish.

1-8; 5:02 pm

Racism is a race everyone is in, but no one wins.

1-14; 9:07 am

Let's call hating what it really is, berating!

1-18; 12:33 am

The only way our outside enemies can win is if they've been given the game plan by us, our foe, or friends.

1-18; 9:23 am

Sometimes being spot on will get us spit on and spat at.

1-18; 9:34 am

Silence is never a solution to solve and win a revolution.

1-18; 3:09 pm

If blackmail is a crime, why are threats I receive if I don't pay a bill written on white mail every time?

1-19; 9:12 am

If someone is blackballed and it's done by someone with white balls, what is it then called?

1-19; 9:16 am

If people are blacklisted, wouldn't it be 'whitelisted' if Wite- Out is used to wipe them off the list as if they never did exist?

1-19; 9:19 am

Was Wite-Out created to cover up and not expose what was written and predated to erase what no one wanted us to know?

1-19; 9:26 am

White-on-white crime, like white pen on white paper, will appear invisible every time.

1-19; 9:37 am

Quoetically Speaking

Black-on-black crime is asinine. Each time, it voids our world of a brilliant spirit and mind.

1-19; 9:39 am

Show me mugshots of modern day crooks, and I'll show you the founding fathers of America who got off the hook.

1-19; 10:25 am

Many get fined for running a stop sign, but what's the fine for failing to stop slave trafficking over a 400+ period of time?

1-19; 10:34 am

We are not racially divided because we've never been united.

1-19; 10:53 am

Black people are like ants; resilient and come back strong even when they've been sprayed & led into traps. They keep marching right along.

1-19; 11:22 am

Everybody doesn't need to be the change they want to see because it's a lot of people who love to hate in our society.

1-20; 8:13 am

Hate escalates death and the heart rate.

1-20; 8:15 am

He that despises the *Behuety* of nature and human kind; must have an inward desire to be blind.

1-20; 8:19 am

Racism makes ass mouch SINce ass diss SINtence. Sense meye pairants tought mea too bee inSINcitive two authers beecuz ov thair culer, eye jus ben leyek diss everr sense.

1-20; 8:23 am

How can we fight and win against the powers that be when they are hiding secretly in government agencies?

1-20; 12:25 pm

How can we expect the judicial system to be fair? Wouldn't that first imply the system has to care?

1-20; 12:26 pm

If we trusted God as many claim we do, many would come to understand there was no mistake when creating most everything with a hue.

1-20; 3:53 pm

Quoetically Speaking

Some cultures are like vultures. They feed off others instead of embracing their own.

1-20; 5:57 pm

This deck of race cards needs reshuffling.

1-22; 8:53 am

The only two races who can play the 'race card' are the reds and blacks. According to all the cards I've seen and been dealt, the white is on their back.

1-22; 8:58 am

Chess, Checkers and Connect Four show you the races who are continuously being unrightfully checked and annihilated in this war.

1-22; 8:59 am

I don't think anyone chose to be in this race that judges the other by their skin and features on their face. What if tolerance of one another was the sole reason we were sent to this place?

1-22; 12:15 pm

The biggest forgery is that we're competing in a race, when the only ones running it are racist who will come in last place.

1-24; 12:20 am

Quoetically Speaking

Most of us didn't sign up for this rat race and that's why we're getting smoke and dust kicked up in our face.

1-24; 12:21 am

Bark as loud as you will, just know barking alone can never kill.

1-24; 1:19 am

Prisons like slavery profits off our melanated seed for greed.

1-25; 7:10 am

It's difficult to decipher an enemy from a friend you once had, when that relationship turns wickedly bad.

1-27; 7:00 am

The line is very thin between enemy and friends. Beware of those who secretly envy you yet grin.

1-27; 7:01 am

We can choose everything else but the skin we're in, even to rid ourselves of hate that resides within.

1-27; 8:22 am

Quoetically Speaking

If heaven is going to be divided by classism and racism to get in, I'll take my chances on change coming in this earthly realm.

1-27; 8:23 am

Even in our race we prejudge based on hair, hues, and features on a face.

1-27; 8:24 am

The real disgrace about racism is it's a race where everyone comes in last place!

1-27; 8:30 am

We get fined and killed for wearing seatbelts or not, hands up or down we still get shot!

1-27; 10:33 am

In an effort to eradicate racism, we will have to radically erase all the racist laws in our legislature's books that systematically allows unfair policies to be written by the same ones who are the real crooks.

1-27; 1:25 pm

Quoetically Speaking

Reflection

Quoetically Speaking

*❝ Race relations is the talk of the hour. Like a relationship gone south; it's stale and sour. We must **fight** against these evils and relinquish its power. ❞*

9
Relationships

Relationships are like ships that will not set sail if we fail to communicate, so we must be intentional who we select as friends and mates

My having standards doesn't mean you stand beneath me. It just means you may not be the one to stand beside me.

1-2; 11:55 am

Being attractive does not guarantee attracting positive *inergy*.

1-6; 12:36 am

Meaningful conversation is like a matchstick. Unless it's struck, no fire will emit.

1-6; 9:02 am

I wish real was a pill.

1-8; 11:57 am

Admittedly, physical attraction is how most relationships begin, but mental connection is where it should blend.

1-10; 8:51 am

I'm moved more by you showing me your character rather than merely describing it.

1-12; 8:48 am

If everyone's yes were a yes, we'd all stress less.

1-14; 9:11 am

Work on getting rid of your addictions, and I'll work on mine. Then as individuals, we'll all be fine.

1-14; 10:52 am

Your looks will never be enough to keep a person who is looking for depth.

1-14; 8:54 pm

Everything you're thinking doesn't need to be said; some things need to be shown instead.

1-16; 9:32 am

You never have to tell anyone you're leaving them. Your absence will say it all.

1-16; 9:51 am

Quoetically Speaking

Favor follows those who do favors for more than just themselves.

1-16; 9:54 am

Your pride will always keep peace outside.

1-16; 7:12 pm

Wait! I asked him to help me tone my weight, not help monitor and judge what I had on my plate!

1-17; 12:04 pm

Truth has many sides but lying to prove your side isn't one of them.

1-17; 1:04 pm

Lying to get others to believe that your word is true, so how's that working out for you?

1-17; 1:07 pm

Come to me with integrity, and you'll always get the best of me.

1-17; 1:18 pm

Show me you're a liar, and I'll show you my inward fire.

1-17; 1:19 pm

Quoetically Speaking

Don't let your disappointments point you in the direction of inaction.

1-18; 7:22 am

Relationships often fail, but don't allow the ones that did keep you in bondage and hell.

1-18; 7:23 am

Relationships are like sailing. You must be prepared with life jackets in case the waves cause you to capsize.

1-18; 8:39 am

Don't misconstrue humility for being able to humiliate me.

1-18; 9:08 am

Supporting someone isn't the same as sporting someone because they hold you up.

1-18; 9:12 am

Am I to construe your silence for lies or the truth?

1-18; 1:59 pm

I'll opt out if you think making me an option is one of your options.

1-18; 2:28 pm

Quoetically Speaking

Oh, how precious is my time! You can devalue yours but definitely not mine.

1-19; 7:25 am

Busy only conveys to me, that I am not your priority.

1-19; 8:15 am

Trying to make some people commit is like trying to make sugar out of shit.

1-20; 12:38 pm

If you want to sex me, you first must undress and lay my mind to rest.

1-20; 12:50 pm

Marriage is a business partnership, nothing less or more, which most fail to execute a business plan for.

1-24; 1:07 am

Feeling your mate with mere hands-like only hearing them will never cause you to understand.

1-24; 1:22 am

A man in love won't have to be told what to do.

1-25; 7:17 am

Quoetically Speaking

A woman in love is easily hurt.

1-25; 7:18 am

Black healthy love is a threat to all mankind.

1-25; 7:20 am

With so many contacts in our phones, why do many of us still feel alone?

1-25; 8:27 am

Many have the appearance of looking like a human being, but not every person is capable of feeling.

1-25; 8:13 am

Seeing you but not feeling you, is no connection at all.

1-25; 8:31 am

You won't learn what is to be learned when speaking out of turn.

1-27; 6:55 am

Is premarital sex really a crime, if marriage is the furthest from one's mind?

1-27; 7:27 am

Quoetically Speaking

Life is but a mere morsel, yet selfish people will take your morsel and eat theirs too.

1-31; 11:22 am

Reflection

Quoetically Speaking

> **Relationships** are like ships that will not set sail if we fail to communicate, so we must be intentional who we select as friends and mates.

10
Religion & Spirituality

Many rely on religion to direct our paths. From birth to adulthood, those belief systems are all we've ever had. We must study to show ourselves approved so that we will not be unwise and considered fools.

Go, be, and do what your spirit leads you to!

1-1; 6:51 am

Being money hungry only means a person is spiritually malnourished.

1-8; 3:51 pm

It is better to be financially broke than spiritually in debt.

1-8; 4:43 pm

If crying makes one weak; then why are there so many Jesus freaks?

1-11; 10:21 am

I've met those who prophesize and those who profit with lies. The latter is who I despise.

1-14; 11:43 am

Quoetically Speaking

If the love of money is the root, the seed must be greed.

1-14; 3:50 pm

Faith is an action word that is shown in what we do. Practice yours and I'll practice mine too.

1-15; 2:02 am

Many of us say we fear the plight of our youth, but most are afraid of telling our youth the truth.

1-16; 9:28 am

People talk about biblical accounts as if they were there to give an account.

1-16; 5:08 pm

Is anyone else fed up with the mess we've been told to bless?

1-18; 12:37 am

Your beginning is a precursor, not a curse to your ending.

1-18; 7:29 am

Flying a plane and being on a plane aren't the same thing.

1-18; 10:12 pm

Quoetically Speaking

The way to start your day is praying to The Most High to direct your way.

1-20; 7:46 am

People say they want to go to heaven but are afraid to die. Is it because you're uncertain if you've been fed a lie?

1-20; 7:48 am

Decide on who and what you give your *inergy* and time to.

1-20; 7:54 am

Faith can't be proven unless you act.

1-20; 12:44 pm

Your tongue doesn't have the power to move me, but it can be used to uplift me.

1-20; 12:46 pm

Some churches are like schools. They breed people who are taught but have never learned. Thus, with lies, they have been fooled because they do not discern.

1-20; 2:47 pm

People will yell that the truth is blasphemy but will whisper lies in your ear.

1-20; 2:53 pm

Were the rulings of separation of church and state put in place to divide the hidden truths from all the lies?

1-20; 3:09 pm

Is it hard to conceive that God may be just like satellite TV; having many stations that are able to speak in many tongues of various countries and nations?

1-20; 3:27 pm

Got God, get built. Got religion, get guilt.

1-20; 3:40 pm

Don't allow anyone to lay hands on you with sweaty or sticky fingers.

1-23; 11:40 pm

Read the red if you really want to know instead of being told what Yeshua was said to have said.

1-23; 11:50 pm

Fault-finders can't find a mirror to see themselves.

1-24; 2:13 am

If only the spiritually in debt could file for divine bankruptcy.

1-24; 9:49 am

Quoetically Speaking

The wealthy will never rid the world of the poor, for their mere presence is what makes the rich keep striving for more.

1-24; 9:54 am

What is deemed right is subjective depending on the subjects involved in the debate.

1-24; 7:25 pm

Some should put repenting on layaway because they've used up all their vouchers and excuses that Yeshua paid the way.

1-24; 7:43 pm

We are more like God than we know. If watered with faith, what we speak, and plant will grow.

1-24; 7:39 pm

Would you trust eating the seeds you've sown?

1-26; 10:09 am

As believers, we must have faith in things our eyes can't see, no one has seen the black hole, yet many believe it to be.

1-26; 10:14 am

No one should have to defend that The Most High GOD exists. I'm thoroughly assured; otherwise I wouldn't be writing this.

1-26; 10:15 am

It takes faith for an atheist to deny that nothingness created the air, birds and stars in the sky. If struck blind who'll bet they'll ask GOD to bring sight back to their eyes?

1-27; 7:07 am

I thought repenting involved asking for forgiveness and turning away from that sin, but we keep repeating the same offense again and again.

1-27; 7:13 am

Do disingenuous people really think they genuinely can't be seen for who they really are?

1-30; 7:18 am

Confirmation generally comes when we are in the company of positive relations and maturation to receive the word.

1-30; 7:22 am

Quoetically Speaking

The Most High only aligns us to our assignment when we show up to class.

1-30; 9:10 am

Christians have been told it's wrong to sue. Correction! The Bible clearly validates getting back what is rightfully due to me and you.

1-30; 10:30 am

Every opposition we encounter is to put us in position to defeat our enemy.

1-30; 11:39 am

Reflection

Quoetically Speaking

66 *Many rely on religion to direct our paths. From birth to adulthood, those belief systems are all we've ever had. We must study to show **ourselves** approved so that we will not be unwise and considered fools.* **99**

11
Time Management

Time is impatient and waits for no one, so be about your business and get the job done.

Time chasers are time wasters.

1-2; 5:17 pm

Like water, time runs, yet it can't be frozen.

1-12; 10:55 am

Time and ocean tides are the two things that stay in motion.

1-16; 5:07 pm

You can begin now or later, but later may not ever come. So, now is just as good as any time to just get it done.

1-16; 10:53 am

Making excuses never makes any changes.

1-16; 12:24 pm

Failing to start will surely guarantee your failure.

1-18; 12:38 am

Failure to begin guarantees you will not win.

1-18; 12:39 am

Stealing my time is the number one crime.

1-19; 7:10 am

My time can't be refunded once spent.

1-19; 7:12 am

Time can never run out; it only runs on and on.

1-19; 7:13 am

Like a rare wine, that's how invaluable and irreplaceable I consider my time.

1-19; 7:15 am

Watch out for time-snatchers. They'll try to catch you off guard.

1-19; 7:18 am

If you don't stay aware of time, it will sneak up on you as if your eyes were closed.

1-19; 7:19 am

If I were the police, I'd fine everyone who wasted my time.

1-19; 7:21 am

People don't mind wasting your time when they have no sense to mind their own.

1-19; 7:22 am

If you give me a time to meet, the only way I won't be on time is if there an unexpected accident on the street.

1-19; 7:27 am

If you manage your own time, you'll never be a slave to someone else's.

1-19; 7:46 am

Time is like something stolen, it can never be returned.

1-19; 7:49 am

I know abusing drugs is whack, but abusing time, there's no rehab for that.

1-19; 7:53 am

I don't have enough time in my day to chase time-wasters away.

1-19; 8:10 am

Those who value your grind will show up on time.

1-19; 8:11 am

If alive, we all get 24 hours in a day and seven days a week. If you find extra time, wherever you're hiding it; let me sneak a peek!

1-19; 8:15 am

A person who never apologizes is the same person who will say, my way or the highway.

1-19; 11:57 am

Master your mind, and you'll master your time.

1-20; 7:52 am

Tired of inaction? Maybe you need to monitor who or what is your distraction.

1-20; 8:04 am

The difference between the haves and the have nots is the money.

1-22; 8:47 am

Quoetically Speaking

The early to rise are few. They are the ones to see and touch the morning dew.

1-22; 11:06 am

We can count the hands of time, but we'll die trying.

1-24; 7:37 pm

Time rolls in like waves. We'll catch or miss the tide.

1-24; 12:03 am

Intent only implies what one intends to do but acting on one's intent is called intentional follow-through.

1-24; 9:43 am

Your time shouldn't be eaten up by gluttonous people who just love to gobble it up.

1-26; 9:59 am

Sponsoring foolishness is a foolish way to waste one's time.

1-27; 2:51 pm

When I leave this place, I'll be in another time in space.

1-27; 2:54 pm

Quoetically Speaking

Confining my mind is like trying to hold time.

1-27; 2:55 pm

Crime doesn't pay with your money it pays with your time.

1-28; 7:47 pm

Look for signs because there's no guarantee you'll have a clock to tell you the time.

1-30; 6:50 am

Day takes breaks for no one, but it will break for the early one who's awake.

1-30; 7:20 am

Just because you don't see the sun rise doesn't imply it's not in the sky.

1-30; 7:21 am

Anticipating the birth of a sunrise, will give your eyes a glorious surprise.

1-30; 7:22 am

Nothing comes to a dreamer who fails to remember to write their dreams down.

1-30; 7:23 am

Quoetically Speaking

Reflection

Quoetically Speaking

66 *Time* is impatient and waits for no one, so be about your business and get the job done. 99

12
Womb-n-Man

We as women have a womb and the man possesses the seed, he needs us, and we need him in order to conceive.

A real woman will always follow if a strong man takes the right path and lead.

1-4; 9:55 am

Mothers are our first teachers on how and what to eat to survive.

1-4; 10:03 am

When he laughed from the gut, I knew he was well.

1-6; 3:08 pm

Even the great die.

1-13; 3:13 pm

Hands were meant to create. Show me your masterpiece.

1-14; 9:03 am

Quoetically Speaking

Resiliency has kept you in the game, so let the world know your name and why you came.

1-18; 7:26 am

Unity can only be when U and I realize like black, red, and brown ants that we're from the same colony and not each other's enemy.

1-19; 8:28 am

Can't make it any clearer, we must first start with the one standing in our mirror.

1-20; 8:06 am

Committing requires submitting to a course of action. If you don't move, there will be no traction.

1-20; 12:42 pm

Since when has a newborn violated any of the 10 commandments? We learned to sin growing up as women and men.

1-20; 2:58 pm

Many will smile all the while driving a drill in your back.

1-22; 8:03 am

It's the ones we least expect who are the suspects trying to get us for all they can get.

1-22; 8:08 am

It's not always the one who works the hardest who wins, but rather the one who works the wisest, my friend.

1-22; 8:18 am

People don't need our pity. They need a plate full of compassion.

1-22; 8:34 am

When we know better, we should show better.

1-22; 9:10 am

We must learn how to act. How to be or not to be, that is what determines our true identity.

1-22; 9:12 am

Do you. Be you. Someone else getting to the top should not stop you from getting there too.

1-22; 9:14 am

Quoetically Speaking

When you follow Master's Decree, that's when you obtain your true master's degree.

1-22; 10:39 am

Surpassing goals you set is like getting extra credit in the class of life.

1-22; 11:37 am

Pressing toward the finish line causes us, with each step, to elevate our minds.

1-22; 11:54 am

The more one thinks, the more they think they're right.

1-23; 11:36 am

We get what we get sometimes without ordering it.

1-23; 11:43 am

Your story can only be truthfully told by you.

1-24; 12:11 am

Pleasing people is like trying to have sex with the world.

1-24; 12:14 am

Quoetically Speaking

Show me the wealthiest person alive and I'll bet they have few friends.

1-24; 12:38 am

Excusing your excuses is never the solution.

1-24; 1:01 am

As a woman, we can't be the wife, mommy, husband and daddy too; we need our men to fulfill what they were called to be and do.

1-24; 1:09 am

My femininity isn't to be misconstrued with my identity.

1-24; 1:18 am

Until we treat each other like kings and queens, we will be used and seen as pawns.

1-24; 2:04 am

A queenly woman will only be captured by a king who is willing to honor and crown her with a ring.

1-24; 2:06 am

The mirror should first judge the reflection it sees.

1-24; 10:42 am

Quoetically Speaking

I don't knock a prostitute's grind; I have a problem with the one who pimps her by screwing up her esteem and mind.

1-24; 1:40 pm

Women, we should never emasculate a man just because we can. We are his legs, they are our feet and without them neither of us can walk nor stand.

1-24; 7:00 pm

How I deliver my words will determine if they are listened to or just merely heard.

1-26; 10:03 am

Love is something we require before we both expire.

1-26; 10:07 am

Let's spare each other with the Peace, Namaste and Ashe, if behind those words you are intending to send negative *inergy* behind what you say.

1-27; 7:32 am

Our bodies are mere temples we were assigned to temporarily assist and serve.

1-27; 8:20 am

Quoetically Speaking

We didn't choose the skin we're in, yet we must accept that it was all by a designed plan.

1-27; 8:21 am

No need to imitate, just embrace that you're great!

1-27; 2:52 pm

Imitators imitate initiators.

1-27; 2:57 pm

Reflection

Thank you for taking the time to read, reflect, and respond by taking note on these quotes.

Other Published Work:
Fo'Ur Seasons-Stories of Poetry 2012
Lessons From My Grandmother's Lap 2018
Available as Ebook on smashwords.com and Print Version on amazon.com

To Order:
Books, T-Shirts & CD's: PayPal.me/itsunl2me
Available for Booking at Various Venues Anniversaries, Churches, College, Conferences, Festivals, Fraternity and Sorority Functions, Graduations, Home Goings, Panel Discussions, Reunions, Seminars, Shelters, Showers, Weddings & more. Also specializes in creating personalized framed name poems and greeting cards.

Contact:
itsunl2me@gmail.com
www.isnatianti.com
Mailing Requests:
PO Box 1638 Atlanta, GA 30012

Booking Information
www.gigsalad.com

Social Media
FB: ITS Unlimited LLC & Isna Tianti
IG: istian.creations
YouTube: Isna Tianti

Special Thanks to all who pre-ordered and patiently awaited the production of this book, I greatly appreciate you and your belief in me and my writings. Gwendolyn C, Winston, Aunt Elaine Williams, Althea Williams, Stacy Douglas, Ronald Love, Kimberly Lawrence, Nona-Kerry Effort-Fouse, Angel Davis, Obadiah Cooper, Bahia Carson, Erica Burton, Lisa Brigham, Montoya Smith and Ahneva Ahneva.

www.ingramcontent.com/pod-product-compliance
Lightning Source LLC
Chambersburg PA
CBHW060353110426
42743CB00036B/2971